See Thru Other People And Know Yourself

by Brian Thomas

Other Books by Brian Thomas

Think for Yourself: Control Your Life

Can Do Exercise Program

Getting Past Me and Being Closer to Thee

I'm Dying to Get to Heaven

Peace of Mind

Published by World Class Promotions

Forsyth, GA

ISBN: 978-1-7372228-2-8

Published in the United States

Introduction

This book is about people, all kinds of people, good and bad, rich and poor, black and white. Each and every one is different, but they all share the same traits. This book is to help you identify the traits and hopefully understand others as well. When you can understand other people, you will be able to understand yourself and vice versa. This is a social world and we must interact with people we come into contact with. How well this interaction takes place depends upon our ability to read people.

Hopefully when you have read and digested this book, your interactions with people will be better. There are a couple of realities that we need to be aware of. The first is that no matter how bad a person is, there is some good in them, and no matter how good a person is, there is some bad in them. The other thing to remember, especially with friends and relatives, is we must accept them as they are, not the way we want them to be. We do not have to accept what they do, but we need to accept them.

This book will not only show you how to read people, it will help you have smoother relations with everyone. There are ways to become a more likeable person, and if you really begin to know yourself and what you are all about, you will wind up liking yourself better, which will lead to a happier life. People are fascinating creatures and become even more so when you see through them.

"All men seek happiness. This is without exception. Whatever different means they employ, they all tend to this end.

The will never takes the least step but to this object. This is the motive of every action of every man, even of those who hang themselves."

- Blaise Pascal, Pensees

Chapter 1

The Answer and the Quest

Our happiness, our life, our fate, and even our fortune is dependent upon our relations with other people and our personal interaction with them. This is all contingent upon knowing and controlling our own nature and being able to "read" other people to the extent that we have an insight into their thinking and their motives involving other people and ourselves. We are all mirrors of others. We can see ourselves in other people and vice versa. Our motives and the motives of others have one thing in common: The very simple but true motive for all is that we are motivated to do what makes us feel good.

If we are in a situation where feeling good is not our primary motive, then we do what is in our best interest. Example: If we are in a life-or-death situation of which feeling good is not an issue, then we do what is in our best interest, which is basically doing what makes us feel good. This is a given. Next comes the big question, why does what we do make us feel good? What makes you feel good and why? We probably can't answer that question for others, and we may not even be able to answer that question for ourselves.

The reason is that almost everything we do is driven by our subconscious mind, which is 90% of our mind. Our conscious mind is only 10% or even less. We use the conscious mind to study and learn new movements. It also governs our movement and willful thought. The subconscious stores away all we have ever learned or experienced, good and bad; this allows us to do things automatically without thinking. It controls the beating our heart and all bodily functions. It is an all-important force that makes us great or makes us amount to nothing. Our subconscious is where the answer lies as to why things make us feel good. You can plummet the depths of your subconscious, maybe, but you cannot go down into the subconscious mind of others.

The good news is that when you are able to get into your subconscious mind, then you will finally find out that a lot of what makes you feel good, also makes the other person feel good. Take a look at a traumatic incident in your life and relive it frame by frame as in a motion picture, and see how each frame makes you feel and what impression it made on your mind. This can be difficult because the pain, guilt, and regret that lies buried in your subconscious will now surface, but you will understand or realize why it makes something feel good in your mind, even if it's nothing but avoiding what's down there in your subconscious.

We rarely refer to the Bible, but in this case it makes a perfect illustration of the subconscious. James 3:6 states, "the tongue is a flame of fire . . . it can set your whole life on fire . . . it is a restless evil, full of deadly poison." This is a true statement, but one vital thing has been left out. A fire needs fuel. If someone speaks with anger or hatred or lies, belittles or insults others, then the fuel comes from their subconscious.

This is basic and just the beginning in the quest to see through others and know yourself.

Chapter 2

Different Directions

Our mind is amazing. Each of us has seven completely different aspects to our personality. They are in operation during all of our waking hours, and some believe that they have an effect on our subconscious mind when we are sleeping. The mind carefully orchestrates, controls, and directs their operation. Most people are unaware of all seven aspects of their personality and how they totally comprise our outward and inward behavior. The aspects that will be discussed in this book are as follows:

1. First Impressions
2. Natural Dispositions
3. Preoccupations, Interests, and Goals
4. Temperament
5. Life Styles
6. Values
7. Past, Present, Future

These aspects work in complete harmony like a well-oiled machine. All of these parts of our personality have a direct bearing on who we are, what we are, and how we think and act. These parts of our personality must contend with the parts of other people's personalities, which can result in conflict or harmony. If someone is aware of each of the different parts of their personality, then they will be able to have more control over their thoughts and behavior.

This book will attempt to put you in touch with yourself and at the same time, give you an insight into the thinking and behavior of others. You will have a choice of whether to react to what someone says or does, or to consider what caused the person to say or do what they did, and then you can think before you say or do something rather than act on initial impression. The choice will be yours, and you will have more control of the situation.

Chapter 3

Direction #1: First Impression

Before we meet or engage with someone, we need to take into account three vital aspects of our psychological make-up. The first is our number one instinct of survival. Next comes our second strongest instinct, which is sexual, and last but definitely not least is our personal ego. We all have one, be it large or small, and it does dominate what we think, say, or do. We always have to ask ourselves the question: Is this my ego talking?

When people meet someone for the first time, something happens that neither one of them is aware of, which determines the course of their relations. Without consciously being mindful of doing so, they put that other person in one of three categories: inferior, equal, or superior to them. The other person is doing exactly the same thing, and neither has any knowledge of what is happening.

When a person regards someone as inferior to them, obviously their ego is in full gear. They may show a certain amount of respect, but in reality, they have little or no respect or regard for the person. They do not consciously take this into account. They are not aware of the way they are coming off. Now, if the other person considers themselves to be superior also, then we have two egos locking horns. This leads to either no relationship or a very tense one with each one on the defensive.

Should the other person consider themselves equal to the person who feels superior to them, the superior feeling person will reject them and no relationship is possible. If a person considers themselves to be inferior to that person, then the person who considers themselves superior will be saying to themselves, "They realize I am superior to them and I will help them or at least be nice to them." This will result in a submissive relationship where the person who feels inferior will be somewhat submissive to varying degrees.

The question then arises of how to deal with a person who considers themselves to be superior to you. The answer lies in the reality of the situation. Is this person powerful or influential, or do they have great wealth, superior talents? Are they a known and famous personality? If the answer is yes to any of the above, regard their accomplishments and treat them with respect, but do not be deferential. If the person is an egoist and nothing more than that, let them play their part and appear to be impressed. The relationship is doomed to go nowhere.

When you meet a person and they consider themselves equal to you, unless you have more or accomplished more than they have, then they are usually a well-balanced person. These people do not idolize people or consider people less who do not have money or much education. They tend to accept people as they are. If you feel equal to a person who considers you equal to them, then this is the best relationship you can have because there is respect, common ground, and harmony. This is the best way to deal with this person.

Next comes if someone feels inferior to you, it's obviously because they have a sense of low self-esteem or worth. They consider you above them for whatever reason. The best way to treat this person is, first of all, with kindness and acceptance and allude to the fact that you are willing and can help them if they so desire. Try to make this person feel good about themselves and encourage them in every way you can.

You now have the advantage of being able to size up the person, know how they feel about you and themselves, and respond to the situation, which they don't even know is taking place. It's all happening right in front of their eyes, but they don't even see it.

The Size Up

When you meet someone for the first time, you have a unique advantage. You realize they are putting you in one of these categories and they don't. Since you are armed with this knowledge, you will be able to know what category they put you in. You have to be aware and ask yourself, do they consider me inferior, equal, or superior? When you ask yourself this question, you will be able to sense how they regard you and act accordingly. You can have total control over the situation and make this first meeting to your benefit. Since you know how they regard you, you can choose to have a relationship or not have a relationship. If you choose to have a relationship, you will know what kind it will be.

Chapter 4

Direction #2: Natural Dispositions

Teachers

hen we speak of teachers, this does not necessarily refer to

W those who teach in a classroom environment. This refers to anyone who has a desire to share what they know with other people. This is a natural inclination and cannot be taught or learned. Teachers for the most part are very sincere people. They usually are willing to share what they feel to be true. When they speak, it's from their heart or from the beliefs they hold, whether these beliefs are popular or unpopular. With teachers, it's what you see and hear is what you get.

There are two types of teachers: Likeable and Irritable.

Likeable teachers all have one thing in common: They are patient and they will listen to other people and actually consider their point of view. They have an innate desire to help others through teaching them something which they do not know. They enjoy the esteem and appreciation shown to them. In a word, teaching others makes them feel good. It satisfies a need deep inside of them to be recognized and accepted. Likeable teachers are usually people persons. Some teachers are very reticent and keep to themselves, but will respond to someone who has a desire to know more. Teachers function best with those who are eager to learn and have an open mind. When dealing with other people, they prefer that it's on an equal basis with the other person.

Likeable teachers are tolerant of others and have a sincere like if not love of people. They have a sense of humor and usually no not take themselves too seriously. They are able to put people at ease and establish a real support system and lend a hand, which inspires people to not only learn, but to excel.

Irritable Teacher

Irritable teachers have a short fuse and a lack of patience. They cannot understand if someone does not grasp what they are trying to convey. They are easily frustrated and prone to show their frustration. They are especially irritable with slow learners. They are more focused on their need to teach than they are on the people who they are teaching. They have a deep-seated desire to impress others with their knowledge and achieve the recognition they feel they deserve. Irritable teachers usually don't like themselves and who they are. Lasting relationships usually elude them. They have a desire to help others, but strictly on their terms. This makes them selfcentered.

The Size Up

Teachers are usually easy to recognize. They are friendly with most, if not all, of people they meet and know. They are usually easy to talk to and tend to be helpful if they can be. They do have a serious side since they feel responsible for dispensing any knowledge of what they know and make sure it is precise and correct. In a word, they are pleasant to be around and you will usually leave with something that you had not known before. These are the likeable teachers.

Irritable teachers, on the other hand, are more intense with less patience and will not accept any contradiction of what they think or say. If you disagree with them or have another point of view, they become very agitated and will likely interrupt and try to "set you straight" in no uncertain terms and not be very nice about it. They become extremely frustrated if they are not able to impress you with what they know. You have to accept them on their terms in order to have any kind of relationship with them.

Chapter 5

Natural Dispositions: Actors

Actors are performers who act out their part to impress people with their strength, intelligence, ability, etc... there is no sincerity, only a desire to be perceived as sincere and react.

Act can be a noun or a verb depending on how you use it. When it's used as a noun, then it signifies that someone is just putting on a show or "act." This is what actors do. It is the lack of sincerity that puts them in the actor category. Acting allows them to retain total control. For example, the head of a collection company once told the collectors that they could act mad, sad, glad, or bad to collect the bill, but they could never actually get mad, sad, glad, or bad. This was telling them that if they became emotionally involved, they would lose control. Actors are manipulators. Their goal is for you to believe them and "buy" their act. There are two types of actors: Likeable and Irritable.

Likeable Actor

Likeable actors are enjoyable to be around since they believe the best way to gain attention is to entertain and gain admiration. They use laughter and good humor as their stock in trade combined with a pleasant and likeable personality. They must remain unemotional since true feeling would distract them from the mission at hand to gain votes, money, sexual favors or maybe just to be accepted, admired, and trusted. The feeling of being "on stage" and drawing people out and turning them on can be almost an addiction. They must be devoid of true personal involvement if they are to accomplish this.

Irritable Actor

Irritable actors have little or no control over their ego and they regard most people as beneath them. They are obsessed with showing others how "special" they are. When someone questions them or is not impressed by them, or doesn't acknowledge them, they can lash out with a verbal or even physical attack. The irritable actor is devoid of any emotion except anger. This is all theatrical, but bad actors can trip over the line unless they get the needed response and believe their own act.

A classic example of this is the episode in World War II when General George Patton had a "shape up the troops" act. One day he tripped over the line believing his own act, became emotionally involved, lost control and hit a solider who was in the sick bay because of his "nerves." Patton became so incensed that this man was in a ward with severely injured soldiers, that he believed him to be nothing but a coward with no right to be there with the wounded men and so he hit him.

The Size Up

The ability to determine whether a person is sincere or insincere must be developed or we will spend our lives being "taken," that is, being taken advantage of. One way to determine is to observe people when they think no one is looking, or see how they act with people where there is nothing to gain or with people of a lower status than themselves, or what they consider lower. A constant change of expression is also a clue. The big question is do they really mean what they say? This can be put to the test or it may come out by events which transpire. Always consider what someone says and does as an act until proven otherwise unless you really know the person.

Chapter 6

Natural Dispositions: Passive Reactor

There are basically two kinds of people, those who make things happen like teachers and actors, and those who let things happen. These kinds of people are what we call passive reactors. They are, for the most part, unconcerned and watch life go by and just let things happen. Their motto could be, "When it happens, it happens." They may wish and dream, but make no effort or very little effort to make their dreams and wishes come true. They are the spectators in life. They are happy to sit in the stands and just watch the game of life. They have carved out their own little niche and are content with little in return for being left alone.

They will talk and answer, but only to communicate. They will usually never engage people. You could never call them "a people person". The passive reactor lacks any animation or excitement. Passive reactors are divided into two categories, the vacant and the happy.

Vacant Passive Reactor

Vacant passive reactors seem unaffected by almost anything. They could aptly be described as a person with their "head in the clouds". They are indifferent to the point that they care little for most people and what happens to them including themselves in a lot of instances with an almost total noninvolvement and lack of concern.

Happy Passive Reactor

The happy passive reactor could be summed up in a well-known phrase, "Happy-Go-Lucky". They go about life with a smile on their face and a pleasant word for everyone. Most people like them because they are harmless, seem well-intended and have no desire for a conflict of any kind. There may be a lot stirring in them, but it doesn't surface, only in an extreme set of circumstances.

The Size Up

The passive reactor is usually easy to discern. We all have a bit of the passive reactor, whether happy or vacant, in us from time to time. It is our "getaway" from our problems and/or the world in general. We can't be blamed if we "tune out" once in a while. We are complex creatures and subject to change like the weather. All of us are very interesting no matter who we are or what we are. That's what makes sizing up people so fascinating.

Synopsis

This direction of teachers, actors, and passive reactors has included the traits of each, so that each can be identified easily, but it isn't that easy because we all are a combination of all three. The personality will be a percentage of each. Someone may be 85% actor, 10% teacher, and 5% passive reactor, or they maybe 60% teacher, 25% actor, and 15% passive reactor. A person may be a percentage of all three one day and the next day the percentage in each group will be different according to their mood and circumstances. Our two basic problems are to try and size them up when we come into contact with them, and to determine what percentage of each one has that day -- the percentage of teacher, the percentage of actor, and the percentage of passive reactor.

The next and biggest problem we have is to discern whether they are sincere, insincere, or they just don't care. If for instance, you believe them to be sincere when in fact they are insincere, this leaves you wide open to be taken advantage of, or if you believe they care when in actuality they don't, you will not be able to depend on them. This can cause you a whole new set of problems when they are not there when you need them.

When doing a size up, you need to know their track record and patterns of action. All emotions must be set aside if you need to know what they are and who they are.

Chapter 7

Direction #3: Preoccupations, Interests, and Goals

Our lives will take a turn toward what we spend our time and money on, what makes us feel good, and the goals we have set for ourselves.

Physical Interest

The physical pursuit involves action, which gives physical pleasure or stimulates physical activity. The main preoccupations of people whose interest revolves around physical pleasures are eating, drinking, sex, luxury and leisure time or just relaxing. People who live this lifestyle care only about constant pleasure, which provides them with instant satisfaction and gratification. The individual whose goals are the achievement of higher levels in sports, running, weight lifting, or physical control will devote themselves to mental and physical disciplines to achieve these aims. These individuals internalize their pleasure and look to their own body for gratification. They are obsessed with their own bodies, skills, and abilities. They focus primarily upon themselves.

Social Interest

The person whose main focus is on family, friends, and people in general are in this category. They are usually called "people people." They get their main enjoyment from other people. Some in this group devote their lives to animals and/or pets. Social individuals go outside of themselves to achieve good feelings and satisfaction.

Material

The materialistic person is mainly concerned about one of two things or both. Material things, cars, clothes, or anything materialistic which appeals to them. They are thought of as "thing people." The other concern is goals. These people live and breathe for goals, which they have a mindset to achieve. They are called "the goal strivers of the world." Most are very successful since the main purpose of their life is the attainment of a dream.

They use their mind to carefully think and outline plans for the accomplishment of what they plan to do. They have the mental disposition to achieve their ends. This includes discovering miracles cures, writing music, excelling in the arts, amassing fortunes, running companies, or directing wars. The other materialist sort sets out to accumulate things and to gain the pleasure that they can from those things. They are sometimes called "shopaholics." Shopping for things becomes a passion to them, to the exclusion of most other activities. Some refer to those in this group as "materialist."

The Size Up

All of us are a combination of physical, social, or material. The question then becomes which traits predominate our actions? The size up is determined by which one takes first place and then which one takes second place. When this can be determined on an objective level, it will give us a true insight into the real bonafide nature of the person.

Chapter 8

Direction #4: Temperament

The size up is akin to look at three coins. Each has 2 sides.
   1. Friendly and Unfriendly
2. Indecisive and Decisive
3. Impulsive and Careful

1. Unfriendly

Observable Characteristics:
  Silent, sullen, cold, morose
  Apparently antagonistic
  Apparently indifferent
  Silently disagreeable
  Resentful
  Detached

This person is careful of you. They may feel their best defense and a way of coping with people and situations is to withdraw. They feel people can outtalk or manipulate them, so they become silent, indifferent, and apparently antagonistic.

Do's --
Talk simply to them
Treat them with dignity and respect
Don't --

Ask them questions
Try to make them talk
Talk too much

2. Friendly

Observable Characteristics:
Smiling
Apparently extroverted
Talkative
Diplomatically disagreeable

This person is very lovely and not only wants to, but needs to, be with people. This would seem to be a paradox, but nonetheless true. They must feel accepted by people and unconsciously realize that being friendly is probably the best and only way to achieve this.

Do's --
Try to keep the conversation going
Don't --
Try to be more friendly than they are

3. Decisive

Observable Characteristics:
Good listener
Confident
Self-assured
Positive and usually egotistical
Feels superior to most
Likes to make their own decision

This person feels that the best defense is a good offense, and they are

on the offense from the beginning. They will immediately assume or try to assume control. This is done unconsciously and automatically. This individual must dominate and have control of other people and situations. Their nature will not allow them to take a backseat to anyone.

Do's --
Let them do the talking
Ask questions
Listen
Don't --
Criticize
Interrupt them

4. Indecisive

Observable Characteristics:

Poor listener

Uncertain and confused

Neglectful and Procrastinates

Mind wonders back and forth

Hidden submissiveness

Dislikes making decision

The above individual lacks confidence in themselves and looks to others to make decisions for them. They try had to avoid responsibility and are easily influenced by others with strong conviction.

Do's --

Realize their limitations

Don't --

Try to make them take responsibility

Try to force them to make a decision

#5. Careful

Observable Characteristics:

Calm, slow, careful

Patient and thorough

Detailed, studied, and concentrated

Likes to make his own decisions but slowly

Good listener

This type of person has been conditioned to analyze and use logic and deduction to arrive at a conclusion or a decision to act. They have a slower type of acceptance and use thoroughness to be assured in his own mind. They are careful of the situation rather than the person and are often referred to as a "pipe smoker."

Do's --

Deal thoroughly with details

Give them time to think

Give them just the facts

Don't --

Push them

#6. Impulsive

Observable Characteristics:

Intense, quick

Impatient
Nervous
Constantly changing trains of thought
Concentrated and active
Likes to make their own decision

This particular person is hard to nail down in a single course of action. They are inclined to be bored easily and seem to be constantly changing directions. They are involved in many different things at one time, and no one knows which direction they are going to take next, not even them. They are like a tornado. You never know when or where it will touch down. They are known for having a "short fuse."

Do's --

Be quick and active in your dealings with this person
Try to be patient

Don't --

Get into specifics until you have dealt with generalities
Become involved in their erratic patterns

Synopsis

The temperament size up can usually be done with the choice of one category. The majority of people will fall into one of the six temperaments, which seem to include most of their characteristics, but doesn't rule out a change in temperament depending on the situation.

Chapter 9

Direction #5: Lifestyle

This classification has to do with patterns of behavior which, have become ingrained and pretty much form a person's lifestyle due to habits formed over the years. These are the three groups:

1. Normal
2. Desirable
3. Neurotic

1. Normal

What is normal? Normal in this sense means conforming to a norm or middle of the road behavior with little or no deviation.

Observable Characteristics:

  Marital accord

  Compatibility with spouse

  Home centered

  Contented (that is pleased and satisfied with what they have)

  Low or medium aspirations for self and children

  Limited interest in social activities

  Job satisfaction

  Little imagination

  Lack of spontaneity and creativity

  Constant and uniform in life patterns

The above individual is happy with what they have and would prefer for their life to progress with as few disturbances as possible.

2. Desirable Person

Observable Characteristics:

  Interests outside of home

  Higher aspirations

  Pronounced interest in social activities

  Open to career changes -- spontaneity

  Active imagination and creativity

  Variable and flexible according to situation

This type of person enjoys life, doing new and different things, meeting and associating with all kinds of people, relates well to others, is keenly interested in their work or career, but always looking to progress, and is not resistant to change if it's for the better. This individual allows themselves considerable deviation from established patterns, but still retains some kind of continuity and balance in their life with active pursuits in many and varied interests.

3. Neurotic

  Observable Characteristics:

  Obsessed with certain ideas, beliefs, and fears

  Full of conflicts

  Responds to situations in a negative manner

  Lack of emotional control

  Reacts before thinking

Guilt
Wishes to escape
Defeated attitude
Lack of confidence
Full of hostility, anger, and resentment
Slow to let go of a grudge
Frustration, hopelessness
Lack of interest and ambition
Bored a great deal of the time

This individual's life is controlled by negative feelings, thoughts, words, and actions. This causes chronic discontentment and unhappiness. This negative attitude is a breeding ground full of obsessions of many and all kinds. Their life consists of instability and they usually wonder from one neurotic obsession to another.

Chapter 10

Direction #6: Past, Present, and Future

We are all living in three time frames at once and most are not even aware of it. Life is basically a giant movement from birth to death. Time is always moving and so are we. An analogy of this could be that life is like a car ride. The past is in the rearview mirror. The present is what we are driving past or through and the future is ahead of us down the road. We are influenced by all three.

We can size a person up if we can become aware of their past experiences, both good and bad, their present anxieties and what presently makes them feel good, as well as their future hopes and dreams -- their wish list for the future, so to speak. All three occupy the mind 24 hours a day. Along with the other six directions in which the mind is also going at the same time, we live in a world that seems to become more complicated and things are moving faster the more time goes on. It's no wonder that we should be surprised that happens considering how each individual interest, in one way or another, comes into conflict with everyone they meet, and actually with everyone else on the planet Earth.

Past Experiences

We amount to a mass of conditioned reflexes. Everything we have experienced in the past, good, bad, and traumatic, large and small, has left an impression on us that can explain a great deal of our behavior. We may not want to go back into the past for a good reason, but make no mistake, it is there. If we truly wish to know who and what we are, we must make that journey into our past and see it for what it truly was. Day after day, we are getting better or worse. Some of us realize it, some don't and some don't want to. Our today is a replay of our yesterday in more ways than we like to acknowledge sometimes. Our yesterday belongs to us and no one else.

Present

Our present is what our conscious mind is aware of from minute to minute. Time never stops and our mind never stops. It is composed of our conflicts, both with ourselves and others, or present anxieties, pain, mental, physical, or both, or our present economic status. We have all kinds of fears, such as health, age, death, and other changes. This is our present and this is where we live.

Future

The future is our great hope or fear. Unlike the past and present, we have no idea what it holds. It belongs to us, but it doesn't belong to us, because in this world we live in, anything can and does happen. We are always looking around the next corner to see what is there. The future prepares us to prepare for anything. One thing we do know is that from birth to death and everything in between, is a choice. We choose to think, act, and react to everything. We will always be three people.

The person we think we are.

The person other people think we are.

The person we are.

There are two basic truths. There is only one good, which is knowledge. And there is only one evil, which is ignorance, and you will never get out of life alive.

Chapter 11

The Influence of Alcohol

This is an unusual and unique way of sizing someone up. When people drink too much or get drunk, part of their conscious mind is repressed and some of their subconscious mind surfaces. The mind is divided into two parts, the conscious and the unconscious. 10% of the mind is the conscious and 90% subconscious like an iceberg where only 10% is above the surface and 90% is below the surface.

Conscious Mind	Subconscious Mind
1. The choice 2. The Will 3. The Awareness 4. The Learning 5. The Suggester 6. Logic	1. Automatic reactor 2. Suggestion acceptor 3. Home of the memory 4. Keeper of the skill 5. Silent computer 6. Garden of ideas -- ingenuity, originality, inventions 7. Dwelling place of the intuition 8. Instigator of the living processes

The subconscious mind determines our fate for better or worse and houses our true personality. When a person drinks or gets drunk, their true personality comes out since the inhibitors of normal behavior have been released. Our true personality resides in the subconscious. The conscious mind projects what we wish people to think of us in order to impress them.

Our subconscious is home to all of our memories, good and bad, some of which have produced conditional reflexes, such as when you hear a word or see something, it brings to mind something that has happened to you either good or bad. You automatically react. This is a conditional reflex and we are a composite of all of our conditional reflexes, which determine who and what we are and how to act and react. When we drink, our inhibitors are released and our true personality surfaces. There are five basic types of personalities that emerge.

#1: The Flirtatious Drunk

This person, male or female, will exhibit repressed sexual desires. They will "come on" to those who they would never do so when sober. They have passion hidden away in their subconscious which comes to light when they imbibe with alcohol.

#2: The Nasty Drunk

This person has a great deal of repressed resentment and grudges that they are holding and have now released. They are very critical and judgmental. They harbor strong negative feelings which are kept under control as long as the conscious mind is in control. They realize it is in their best interest to restrain themselves.

#3: The Sad Drunk

Those who are subconsciously depressed about any number of things; the death of someone close, a storehouse of regret, or the way their life has turned out and is presently going, "let it all out" and can't hold back the miserable, despairing, dismal feelings they have. It becomes a flood of despondency. They have lost all control and their sorrowful emotions take over.

#4: The Happy Drunk

No one can make the happy drunk mad. All words of anger or disgust have absolutely no effect. A happy drunk will just laugh them off, free of care and any desire to be accepted and liked by others. They have a need to be free from all constraint society has placed upon them and basically reject fitting into any kind of mold which will make them socially acceptable.

#5: The Mean Drunk

The mean drunk is different than the nasty drunk in that the nasty drunk is critical and judgmental. The mean drunk has intense anger and hatred buried in his subconscious. They will say and do things, which are meant to hurt others mentally and or physically. They get a feeling of satisfaction from this that in a way satisfies their subconscious anger and hatred. It should be no surprise that the meek and silent among us will become this way when the alcohol takes over.

Example -- A True Story

There was a man who owned a trucking company with 13 employees in the office. One of the employees sat at a desk in a corner of the room. He had a job that required a great amount of paperwork. He was very meek and mild mannered. He seldom spoke or had any conversations with the other workers.

One year, the owner decided to have a Christmas party. He had the event catered and provided all kinds of drinks, including alcohol. The man who sat in the corner and who kept to himself all year began to drink whisky until he became very drunk. After he had too much to drink, he went up to the owner in a very angry mood and began to call him all kinds of nasty names. He then proceeded to attack him physically. He had to be restrained by four other men in the office who he also started to cuss at, and then he was physically abusive to the men who tried to restrain him. This is a classic example of repressed feelings which came to the surface once the inhibitions were released by alcohol.

Synopsis

Some drunks may be a combination of two types such as a happy and flirtatious drunk, or they may evolve into another type of drunk such as how a nasty drunk may become a mean drunk. All kinds of things happen when the dynamics of the subconscious are let loose and set free. Each one of us is completely different since we all have had different experiences in life, which has determined our conditional reflexes. We are a mass of conditional reflexes with no one having the same set of conditional reflexes.

Chapter 12

Values

What do we value and how much do we value it? And what do other people value and how much do they place a value on it? We all have different values. That's what makes up our personalities and how we think and act. Most people do this and never give it a thought. It's something that is taken for granted. Such as if you know, you know. There are at least sixteen areas that people place a value on without hardly realizing it, but they do exist and they do influence our thinking and our lives. What we value may come into conflict with what other people value and vice versa. We are basically what we value.

16 Values

1. Money, possessions, wealth

2. The Mind
3. Deeds
4. Occupation, line of work
5. Family
6. The lives of others
7. Humanity
8. God
9. A person's words
10. Themselves
11. Uniqueness
12. Example
13. Spirit
14. Experiences
15. Knowledge
16. Power

1. Our value in wealth and possessions

Some people judge a person by the money they have or don't have and the possessions they have or don't have. This is a very shallow assessment of a person when their value is determined by what they have or don't have in personal wealth.

2. The value of our mind

There are those who use their mind and those who don't. People will consider someone "smart" or "not so smart." They will have little or no respect for those that don't.

3. The value of our deeds

When someone commits an act, it will be positive or negative. When all of these acts are combined, they will have a value. The value of a person's deeds is usually determined by the deeds of the person who is judging them. If their deeds tend to be negative, they will be accepting of a person who commits negative acts. If it's a person who does positive deeds, the person will only respect those who act in kind. Birds of a feather flock together.

4. Our value of our work

People are judged by the kind of work they do. We all have to work and that work can be skilled or unskilled. Skilled work could be a plumber or a doctor, etc... Unskilled could be a laborer or dishwasher, etc... The kind of work people do will determine to a large degree as to what value they are in the eyes of others. This has nothing to do with the value of a person as a whole, but it is one of the ways others are viewed.

5. Our value to our family

This could be called family values. We either place a value on our family or we don't and the way other people value their family will determine what we think of them. We will put them in a positive or negative place depending on how they value or treat their family.

6. The lives of others

Each one of us has a value to our life. When we speak of the lives of others, we are speaking collectively. The question arises, how do we value the lives of others in general? There are those who place no value on the lives of others so they feel free to use those lives for their own benefit or for the benefit of large organizations. Most people do put a value on the lives of others. This can depend upon which category the person designates such as race, creed, or color.

7. The value of humanity

We place a value on humanity in general, meaning all of the people in the entire world. All of the people on earth have a value. We can choose to have a regard for all of humanity or simply not to care and never give it much thought. Caring people will choose to believe that humanity in general has a great value.

8. The value of God

God is viewed in several different ways. People of all religions will value God as the center of their life, while others have a belief in God, but place no specific value to God. The people who do not believe in God cannot place a value on God because for them, God does not exist.

9. A person's words

There is a saying, "He is a person of his word." This of course means that when he speaks and gives you his word, you can rely on it. The words a person speaks have value depending upon the character of that person. Should a person be of low character, his words will have little or no value. People will not listen to what he says. If a person is egotistical and the only words that come out of his mouth are about him, then these words have little value. The only words of value are those which contain wisdom, knowledge, and are positive in nature.

10. People value themselves

Each of us place a value upon ourselves. We may feel we have little value and even consider ourselves worthless, or we can overvalue ourselves and believe we have more value than others and place a high value on ourselves. Most people put a value on themselves for what they contribute to their family, friends, jobs, and perhaps people in need.

11. The value of uniqueness

Unique, strictly speaking, "means being one of a kind" and does not mean unusual. Therefore, a person who is truly unique has a great value because since they are only one of a kind, they are special. The value of a unique person cannot be measured because there is nothing to evaluate them by. It depends how someone looks at a unique person. It can depend upon whether that person is unique in a positive or negative way. It also depends on the intelligence of the person who is placing the value on the uniqueness.

12. The value of example

You can either set a good or positive example or you can set a bad or negative example. The good example has a value of its own because it can have a positive effect on another person's life. Never think that the example you set will go nowhere. It does and it can have a great value to another person and their life.

13. The value of spirit

Who would think that something you cannot see, feel, or taste would have any value? We all have a spirit. Some believe we don't or there are some who attach no meaning to it. Our spirit is the life within us. When we die, our spirit leaves us. Since our spirit is the essence of our life, it must have a value. Its value to us lies in how much we can appreciate it and go within ourselves to be in touch with it in some way. Those who attempt to do this put a value on it and become "spiritual people."

14. The value of experience

The experiences of our life have great value to them because of the lessons we have learned from them to make our lives a little better. Even bad experiences have a value if we can learn something from them. Who can put a value on experiences of being loved? We cannot even begin to calculate the value of that experience. When we learn to put a value on each experience that we have had, the total sum and value of these would astound us.

15. The value of knowledge

The value of knowledge can benefit us in many ways. Knowledge can bring us money, fame, happiness, peace of mind, good relationships, friends, and power. Providing we have acquired knowledge through education or experiences, there can be no doubt that it is of value.

16. The value of power

You can't see power, but you can see the results of power. Power has the value we can't estimate because it gives us an advantage over people and situations. Those who do have power, whether it be physical, mental or political, value that power. It contains value because it makes the difference between success and failure. Therein lies the value. Those with no power realize that it does have value because they have seen what power can do.

Synopsis

What we treasure is what we put value on. What we value is where our heart is at. When you know what a person values, you will begin to see through them and who they are. There are more than 16 values, but these touch on all aspects of life. We all need to look inside of ourselves and be honest with ourselves as to what we truly place a value on. It is not easy to do an introspection since we may have to look at things about ourselves that we may not want to admit. We need to truly know ourselves before we can know other people and we need to know other people before we can know ourself. We must accept ourself as we are and we must know and accept others as they are, but we do not have to accept what they do. We human beings are the most amazing, fascinating, creations on the face of this earth.

Chapter 13

Helpful Hints on Gaining a Rapport and Having Harmonious Relationships

1. Always maintain a positive attitude inside and outside. It will come across when you do.
2. When you meet someone, greet them like they are a long-lost friend that you have not seen in a while.

3. Try to take the word "I" out of our vocabulary.
4. Do more listening than talking.
5. Use their name as much as possible.
6. Always smile, when you do, they will, too.
7. Find something to compliment them about. There is always something that you will be able to compliment them on.
8. Have the attitude that you are no better than anyone, different but not better.
9. Ask questions and seek their advice on the area of their expertise.
10. Talk about them, don't talk about you.
11. Talk about their interests, not yours.
12. If they talk about their problems, don't talk about yours.
13. People like to be around individuals who make them feel good.

The Key to Happiness

Our happiness and success depend upon our ability to have harmonious relationships with others and the choices we personally make. Unless we are intimately aware of who we are, our strong and weak points, our lives will become more difficult. Our relationships with people will depend on how we act and react to them. Our peace of mind comes from knowing ourselves and individuals inside and out. This includes our mate, family, friends, business associates, and strangers we meet for the first time. This book will allow you to really see, maybe for the first time, who you are and see through those around you for who they really are, not the way they wish the world to perceive them.

Conclusion

The better we are able to understand other people and what "makes them tick" will make our life a lot smoother and free us from having problems we don't need. We also must be at peace with ourselves and have harmony in our mind. Our state of mind will depend on knowing who we are, the good, the bad, and the ugly. We must know ourselves for who and what we are. The person we should never lie to is ourselves. An honest evaluation and introspection of ourselves will present us with a problem. Either accept yourself for who you are, or change things you don't like about you. Most of the time, you can't change others, but you can change yourself. You have the power over you. Hopefully this book has let you see inside of others and yourself. The purpose of this book was to do just that.

Helpful Hints on Gaining a Rapport